COMMON SENSE for COMMON GOOD

Change Ourselves – Change the World

• Karen Olson Johnson •

ISBN: 978-0-9819860-7-4

Library of Congress Catalog Number: 2010934417

Printed in the United States of America
Interior pages are printed on recycled paper using 30% post-consumer waste

First Printing: September 2010

14 13 12 11 10   5 4 3 2 1

Edited by Kellie M. Hultgren
Book Design by Christopher Fayers

AMBER SKYE
PUBLISHING

1935 BERKSHIRE DRIVE
EAGAN, MINNESOTA 55122
651.452.0463
WWW.AMBERSKYEPUBLISHING.COM

To order, visit www.ItascaBooks.com
or call 1-800-901-3480. Reseller discounts available.

These Are the Stories . . .

Acknowledgements

The clarity needed to write these words of thanks came to me during the funeral services of a man who had lived across the street in our old neighborhood. Jerry's family and friends gathered in a Legion Hall-type room on the east side of town. Under a fluffy, fabric-draped, and twinkle-lit ceiling that looked like it came straight out of a 1980s prom movie, we remembered our times spent with Jerry.

That room and the folks gathered there represented and reminded me of that for which I am most grateful—relationships—for it is relationships that chronicle our lives. When all was said and done, what was Jerry is what was in that room. We are the sum total of the relationships that we have made in our often very short lives.

With that in mind, I am grateful, profoundly grateful, to my parents, family, and friends both near and far for sharing this earthly time with me. All that I am or hope to be is rooted in their love and within our relationships.

The people in this book of observations have colored these pages with their realities—an existence that the reader now gets to view. I am grateful for experiences we shared and the examples they have been for me. I hope to share with you some of their essence and soul in these pages.

There are special people I wish to thank. Barb's unwavering support was both inspiring and humbling. She sacrificed many hours of personal time and offered to me a level of expertise that made the production of this manuscript magical. In her, I have found a lifelong friend of immense heart.

I am grateful to Lucy for her lasting and continuous support so grounded in love. I find myself wondering what I ever did to deserve such a friend. In every endeavor I have ever undertaken, she has been the quiet strength of an unwavering resolve that has continuously lifted me to a better place.

Judith Palmateer, who as my publisher, has been immensely informative and supportive. As my friend, she is a profound blessing.

This manuscript became a fully orchestrated work through the incredible design talents of Chris Fayers. He is a generous man of great insight and heart, and I am very grateful he shared these qualities with this project.

And finally, my husband, who is my soul mate and has been constant in love and support. The probability that we would meet was unlikely. The probability that we would fall in love, well, was unimaginable. His steady presence and strength in my life, his kindness, generosity of spirit, and humble nature inspire me to grow daily. I would neither be who or where I am today, had it not been for him.

I am grateful to all who made this book become a realized dream.

Truly, our relationships define us. When all is said and done, they *are* what will outlive us.

Preface

Every once in a while a book is written which has the potential to change our world. This is that book.

Common Sense for Common Good provides a realistic way forward through our chaotic world. Looking through the lens of reality, engaging true-life stories draw us all into a better way of life. The problems of our lives and of our world are huge, even daunting. However, you will find plausible and very workable solutions suggested in these pages. If we hold up the lens of self-examination, we will find real ways forward.

This is a book for our time and for everyone. Easily digested in small sections or in one sitting, this is a book all can and should read, probably re-read. This is a book you will want to give to friends and family. It provides inspiration for real change.

What issues does this book address? No less than poverty, global climate change, hunger, charity, justice, conservation, education, and greed to name a few and all in approximately one hundred pages.

Truly, this *is* a book for our times. It provides a real way forward.

Introduction

O ne of the greatest philosophers who ever lived once stated, "The life that is unexamined is not worth living" (Plato, quoted by Søren Kierkegaard). It seems that there have existed identifiable periods within which people re-examine life. Historically, these times have morphed our world into what we see today. The resulting changes, some forced down our throats, some more readily accepted than others, have also made us the people we are today.

We are poised on the brink of another of these times. It is as if we are pushing a giant global reset button. What was accepted as the norm, only recently, has now been brought into question. This planetary unrest is not easy to live through for we are human—humans who loathe change. We do not morph easily. In fact, we do it kicking and screaming.

Every sector of our existence has been called into question in the last few years. Realistically, we can no longer count on what we thought was "truth." It's as if the truth was never true to begin with. Our economy, the environment, our government, indeed the very frameworks of our lives have been, at the very least, misunderstood by us and, at the most, an all-out lie.

All of this uneasiness forces us into the quandary of change. Change that is drastic and maybe painful. Change creates stress, and in an already stressful time, we don't need more.

All of this imposed change leads us to an examination of the status quo. If we are being forced to look at our world and examine what we perceived to be true, perhaps we are really being asked to search for truth—real truth. Through such deep examination, we may finally move closer to what is authentic.

Changes—small changes at that—based on what are real truths do not have to be feared. Such change does not create stress, but alleviates it. Changing a few small things over time, when multiplied by huge numbers of individuals doing it, can create significant results. Lasting results mean a different world for all of us—a world really predicated on truth. How different our world could be if we all worked together! While this concept seems simple, it is truly challenging and ultimately freeing.

The real stories that follow are offered as examples of how we can in fact live a different kind of life than we are now living. No one in this book is famous, wealthy, or out of the ordinary in any way. That's exactly the point. These quite ordinary people have made what seemed like minor changes in their lives and attitudes. By doing so, they changed their lives. The lives of those around them were changed as well.

The focus of this book is on observation. In each of these stories, we are invited into a situation, given a bird's-eye view, and then shown a lesson the situation might teach us.

This book is not a little "green" book filled with the how-to's of a sustainable lifestyle. However, *some* of that information is within these pages.

This book is also *not* a religious book. It does not espouse the virtues of one religion over another, although very strong spiritual themes run throughout.

What this book is, is a book for our times. It contains many examples of ways to move out of the mess that we find ourselves in. These lessons come from our past, from family, from friends, and from my own experiences. Hopefully, these lessons will move us toward profound change.

We must push the reset button, work to bring about a paradigm shift, make life-altering choices. The changes the people in this book made can be ours too. It is that simple, and it can be our future path. What kind of life could we be living if we all worked at it together? What if we all embraced simple truths of a life that is worth living—a life examined and then changed, really in very small ways? It is that profound, it is that true, and it is that simple.

> **"There are times in the lives of all people of conscience when the truth in one's heart is in such deep opposition to the falsehood of the world that one must put everything else in life aside and act upon the truth."**
>
> *Sue Frankel-Streit*

The First One Up

 **charity**   a falsehood of sharing

 **interconnectedness**

fundamentally misunderstood reason and true explanation of our planetary distress

equity   the core notion of global justice

 **simplicity**   **inversely proportional to the unequal distribution of resources in today's world**

My dad used to tell a joke about his time growing up: "The first one up in the morning was the best one dressed." It was Depression-era America in a family with nine kids living in Ashland, Wisconsin. This small town is located on the shores of what can be, in winter, a very cold and harsh Lake Superior. Their small home was heated by a coal stove, often stoked by coal chunks that had been gleaned from what fell off the train cars as they went through town.

Those were hard times. I can only imagine how family life was when parents struggled to feed their children, let alone clothe them. Hence, the joke. If you got up first and ran to the black stove to heat your backside, there, too, was the family selection of clothing. Knowing my grandmother, these would be freshly washed and polished up for the best appearance possible. But pickin's were slim. You put on the clothes, grateful for their warming presence on a frigid January morning with actual temps sometimes thirty degrees below zero. Of course, my dad always added that they had to walk to school. Even in May, you got the impression that their path was through six-foot drifts of snow while facing fifty-mile-an-hour winds.

They learned to share and not to waste anything. He told stories, too, about fixing a pair of shoes that were way past the point of no return. Everything from cardboard, a luxury, to multiple layers of newsprint became inner soles to boost the wearing time of shoes past their prime.

For a lot of us in this country and others like us, we know nothing of a life like this except through stories of our parents and grandparents and, sadly, those reminders are being lost with their generation. Many people in many parts of the world, however, still live as we did during the Great Depression. We now think of them as poor and destitute and in many ways far removed from us. Historically, we were them not so many years ago.

We in America, who consume about 25% of the world's fuel resources, are past, for the most part, that kind of a life. Still, sadly, many in our country are not. For most in the world, struggle is a daily reality. Why is that? How did we get to where we are now?

Some of our post-Depression growth in consumerism, material gain, and wealth was simply a function of the times. The economy was booming with the trappings to show for it. We no longer had to suffer and go without. We had the buying power because of a strong economy to get not only what we needed but also what we wanted. At this point in our country's short history is where the paradigm really shifted and we became a different people.

Here is where we began a gradual thinking shift from desperation and need to comfort and want. If I want it and have the money for it, by golly, I am going to get it! Our consumerism fueled the production of goods unparalleled at any previous time. Our country grew as a mecca for all seeking the good life. The American dream, or nightmare, was born. All that you desire is at your fingertips, at your immediate beck and call, and at a store near you.

There was a paradigm shift to a post-WWII euphoria of life in America. Growth beyond our dreams defined in never before imagined ways. It could have been a very different paradigm. The *choice* we made to go down this road of consumerism and materialism has had consequences—some not yet known and some beginning to surface on a global scale.

It is becoming apparent now that we cannot sustain such an egocentric view of life filled with immediate gratification of desires for a few. Maintaining such an outlook has had the result that the majority of our world's population is suffering.

Think of it this way. On a planet of limited resources, if we consume more than our share, how does it affect the rest of the whole? If you understand that everything is connected, how does a whole group of people who has stockpiled more than they need affect those who do not have enough? Look at our current notion of charity and it may become clearer.

Charity has long been held as a mark of goodness in folks. If you have a great deal, or even if you have a little, it is good to give some of it away. This shows you think of others, not just of yourself. Where the notion of charity goes awry is in the false thinking that it is yours to give in the first place. The universe, God, our planet, whatever you want to call it has a finite amount of resources for a finite number. No one disputes the fact that we find more resources all the time and that we are finding better and more efficient ways to deliver these. However, we never, ever have quite enough for everyone, everywhere.

The problem is in not understanding this principle. If you have, you have because you have been gifted with it. What you perceive as your ability to get more with your talents, abilities, drive, intelligence is also a gift. If we truly believe that everything is a gift and is meant to be treated as such, we need to demonstrate this understanding by how we act. In this way, charity no longer exists. Charity is a negative term.

Illustrate it this way. In my dad's family of eleven (nine kids, two parents), let us assume for argument that he was the strongest, smartest, and most hardworking of the bunch. Often these adjectives are used to describe America as well as those who are "successful." Because Dad personified this in his family, he is given 25% of the family's resources. He eats his fill, wears the best clothes, and sleeps in the softest bed. You get the picture. He is treated with preference and the others get to share what is left over. One with 25% of the pie while ten have 75% which means they each get 7.5%. How could this be seen as just? We all know that every kid in a family should be seen as an equal blessing, regardless of how they look or what their skills or level of intelligence are. All should be nurtured equally to achieve their potential.

That is not the way of the world. Not all are nurtured equally to achieve potential. Life on our planet is based on an uneven distribution of resources, predicated on an immoral sense of justice, and established upon unjust values placed in such things as country of birth, gender, religion … you fill in the rest. Moreover, this concept of justice is supported by our mistaken concept of charity. Those who have an unequal and larger share will "give" some to others.

Our post-Depression consumerism running rampant on our planet has created a mess of such massive proportions we can't even look at it. To examine what has happened means we must look

What does it mean to be part of a family? Part of a global family?

deeply into our own souls. We need to delve deep into areas we cover up with accumulation of wealth, huge closets filled to overflowing with clothes and shoes worn once or not at all, homes with rooms and space never used or used to house more and more stuff, and layers of excess that cover empty hearts unwilling to see how their own overconsumption means less on the plate for the rest.

Is America the first one up to the plate on the planet? Does America deserve to eat up one-fourth of what is on the plate while the rest of the world lives on the remaining share?

The paradigm shift that could have happened post-WWII might have been this. Instead of the thinking that made my father's generation work to acquire material wealth never seen before and to accumulate more than we could ever possibly use, filling our wants and not just our needs, what if we had filled our needs, stopped, and then looked to filling the needs of our global brothers and sisters? Instead, we filled our needs—and our wants—and then only wanted more.

It is not too late. We can peel off our own layers of excess and get to the soul that is the one we all share. When we are at *that* soul, we will see ourselves as part of a large family, a family where everyone gets his or her fair share. This form of supreme justice is the one in which all resources are for all to share. Charity then becomes a word no longer part of our vocabulary. Charity is a misnomer. It implies that something is yours and you choose how and when to give it. With true justice, there is no charity, because everything is shared equally with all.

Like John Lennon wrote, could we imagine a world of no possessions?

So, where do we start? If you have too much, start *giving* it away. Look for opportunities to make a difference. If it's little stuff, like too much clothing or too many shoes, the possibilities are endless as to where to give them. If it is big stuff,

> "When shall we have the courage to outgrow
> the charity mentality and see that at the bottom
> of all relations between rich and poor
> there is a problem of justice?"
>
> *Dom Helder Camara*

like extra houses or cars or property, sell it and feed some people with the money. We have much more than we will ever need, and we can live with less. Well, a lot of us should.

Can the child who will die today because of starvation live with less?

The paradigm could have been different; it was not, but it is not too late to change the world.

We must think of ourselves as part of a larger global family. When one in our family has need, the others sacrifice. We have not been so willing in the past to do this. Taking care of each other in our human family is taking care of a part of the planet. Maybe a more equitable distribution of resources among those on the planet will mean a more peaceful, joyful planet.

Just because you're the first one up doesn't mean you have to be the best one dressed.

World of our "now"

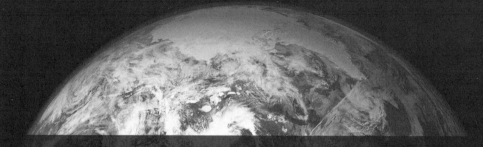

"One out of three people in Sub-Sahara Africa suffers the pain of hunger."
Bread for the World

World of our "new"

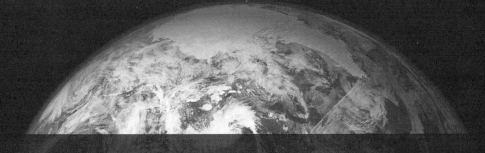

Absolutely *no one* is hungry, and we have lost all the diseases associated with excess.

Can I Come to Your Party?

 **convenience** the moral equivalent
of laziness

 **refuse** another "re" term for our
vocabulary, in addition to
recycle, reuse, retrofit, and so on

 **trash** the accumulation of
convenience

 **non-toxic** does not leave a trail
to follow

S ummer, a short outdoor season for some of us, always means outside parties and gatherings. The smell of wood-fired heat is almost instantly replaced with the smell of grilled meat. With those parties comes the backyard barbecue or grill-fest, and it seems once the season starts so, too, does the use of disposables. Disposable everything: plates, glasses, cutlery, bowls, pans, wrap, napkins, bottles, cans, and bags. You name it and it can be bought and then thrown away. Where does it all go when the parties are over?

Some years back, while teaching high school science, my class performed an experiment on one of these very disposables. We buried a paper plate and a plastic plate in the fall of the year after spending some class time discussing new, time-saving conveniences. Back in that day, the advertisers of the plastic plate shared with us its qualities that included a basically indestructible nature and a claim that plastic would last forever. We put it to the test, and long after the students had forgotten that we had buried the two plates, we dug them up in the spring of the same school year. With basic theory in hand, that being the "good" qualities of plastic winning out over paper, we examined our results. The paper plate was indistinguishable, having disintegrated or decomposed into about half-inch to one-inch chunks of paper. These small pieces crumbled in our fingers as we tried to remove them from the dirt.

The plastic plate, on the other hand, was nearly perfect and, when washed up in the lab sink, looked almost exactly like the photo of the plate taken in September of the previous year. The plastic plate had won out. All hail the plastic plate! The wonders of science—to have invented an indestructible plate! Go away, you lowly paper plate. We have found your replacement—or so we thought. Well, that was then, this is now.

Our understanding of recycling and especially of plastics has changed dramatically over these last few decades. Although some types of plastic are recyclable, plastic is not truly a pure recyclable because most plastic will never again become the first form in which it appeared. That plastic bottle will become a lesser form and perhaps end up in carpeting or in "wood" fencing or decking material, for example. That is, if it is recycled.

Some estimates are that seven or eight out of every ten plastic bottles are never recycled. These bottles end up in landfills and in many other locations. Moreover, remember the plastic plate? They do not break down—or so we thought.

We now know that plastics are not inert. They react with their environment and give off substances, some of them toxic, which may get into the air or water and cause harm to living things. Plastics react with their environment at some time in their life cycle; some plastics are more reactive than others. And plastic takes a *very* long time to degrade. This very substance, prized for longevity in use, will be around for a very long time to clog up our planet. If you buy it and throw it out, it will be around for, well, some might say forever. It will outlive you. Might we begin to think about

How can we make our gatherings more of a celebration for all of us, including the planet?

our adopted, convenience-based attitude, our plastic thoughts, in a new way? For the cost of all that plastic cutlery over the years, one could probably have purchased a nice set of stainless, or better yet bought some unmatched stuff at some thrift store or garage sale. Besides, the unmatched cutlery adds to the informal party and backyard barbeque ambiance anyway.

Do the same for your dishes, glassware, and–oh–napkins. How about real cloth ones? Just imagine. Too expensive? Make some from old tablecloths or fabric remnants. You will have them for years to come. Instead of throwing out plates or plastic glasses or napkins, you have reused and repurposed and basically, well here it goes, saved a piece of Planet Earth. Serve beverages that are in aluminum cans or glass bottles and recycle them. Glass and aluminum are recycled right into … you guessed it … glass and aluminum.

Some of my friends tell me that they eat with disposables all the time because they find it's too much of a hassle to do dishes. We all know that this is not good resource usage and bad for the environment. Perhaps if we had a global "pay as you throw" program, folks would think longer and harder about what we call "trash." South Korea as a nation and even some towns here in the Unite States have adopted such a notion. Recycling and composting are strongly encouraged, and what has to be thrown out is paid for by weight or volume. Such programs obviously cut down on waste because of the connection with money. If we had to pay for everything we threw away, imagine what reuse ingenuity might ensue. It's something to think about.

Part of me wants to bring a real plate, knife, fork and spoon, cloth napkin, and real wine glass to my next invite. I may not be invited again, but I may also open up some conversation, help educate a few folks, and maybe get all of us to act more consciously. Worth a risk? Can I bring my own real fork to your party? Better yet, can we please use real stuff and save the plastic and the planet?

> **"Don't blow it—good planets are hard to find."**
>
> *Quoted in* Time *Magazine, original author unknown*

Small individual choices . . .

Ever-expanding toxic trash piles of a convenience-based existence.

. . . Large collective gains

Zero-waste generating get-togethers and more room on the planet to party.

Are You Thirsty?

mindfulness — thinking past the immediacy of personal gain

limitation — the realization of which results in behavioral change

preservation — real resource recognition translated to personal choice and action

thirst — the result of scarcity

O n a recent early morning trip to the airport to drop off my aunt who'd been in town visiting my mom, I observed a phenomenon that must occur multitudinous times across this country every day. I arrived at my mom's by 4:15 A.M. to pick them up and did not notice it on the way to her house, but on the way back home to mine at about 5:30 or 6:00 A.M. I was amazed by what I saw along the side of the road. On the short drive between my mother's home and my home, I observed eight sprinkler systems watering grass along the roads. For every single system, all with multiple sprinkler heads, there was at least one sprinkler, and in some instances more than one, that was watering the road or the driveway near the sprinkled property. A couple of passes through one sprinkler in particular would have been the equivalent of one of the car washes for which you pay dearly these days. What came to mind?

"What a waste of water!" "There ought to be a law!" Give one, maybe two warnings and then give a citation with a fine. Better yet, give a fine and a watering suspension. We have become so used to seeing green growth that even during our drought-stricken years in the state of Minnesota, we come to expect it, even demand it. We pull up to our favorite restaurant and expect not only our favorite menu items but a big green lawn. If it is brown, we think owners are being irresponsible, not taking care of things. We have come to expect green grass, but at what cost?

We have here in the United States, by most measures, some of the safest drinking water on the planet. For most of us, it is only a small part of our monthly budgets. Imagine if, like most of the rest of the world, we had to pay much more for our water, that it was unsafe to use, or even worse, if we had to walk very long distances to retrieve it.

U.S. citizens use about seventy gallons of water per person per day on just the stuff we do inside. Add all our outside activities and you need to factor in many more gallons. This precious resource is a much taken for granted aspect of life in this country. Considering that less than 1% of the water on the planet is safe for human use, and most people on this planet do not have ready access to potable water, we are a lucky country.

Can my resource use affect someone else?

Lucky and not thinking ahead. As we build more and more and remove more and more trees—those natural water processors—and plant more and more green lawns—those water guzzlers—we hamper the Earth's natural abilities to process this precious commodity. Add global climate change, increasing droughts, and something as simple as the bottle of water you just drank, and the recipe for disaster is starting to cook.

One of the easiest things we can do is to just be aware of and cut down on our personal water use. Shorter showers, low-flow toilets, not letting the water run before or during things like getting a drink or brushing your teeth are simple changes. But such mindful choices can make a huge difference. Oh, and unless you are trekking off into the desert wilderness or a country where the water is questionable, don't drink bottled water.

I asked a woman with a cart full of bottled water at our local big box store, "Where are you going on your trip?"

She responded with a puzzled look and said, "Nowhere."

I asked what was the reason for all the bottled water, and she proudly answered that she and her husband drank only bottled water because she knew it was better for them. Knowing that the particular brand she had in her cart had come from a city water system just a few states away, I thought about asking her why she was willing to pay for water that was the same as what came out of her tap at home. It might have been filtered at the bottling plant. However, by adding a filter to her tap at home, she would basically have the same item. On top of it, she would not have to deal with the forty-eight empty plastic bottles.

What is it? We have been convinced that, because it is in a bottle and transported from somewhere else, it is better than what we have at home. How does the saying go? "Fool me once, shame on you; fool me twice, shame on me."

Bottled water is like the wizard behind the curtain who gives you something you yourself really had all along. The question is why are we willing to pay for it? For about a buck's worth of bottled water, you have the equivalent of four thousand sixteen-ounce bottles of your home tap water. Wouldn't a better use of the financial resources be to provide potable water to those on the planet in need of it for survival? According to World Vision, a child dies every twenty seconds because of water that is unclean.

Please do not take our easy access to water for granted. Reduce the amount of water you use inside and outside your home. Protect this precious resource. Get a filter and fill a safe, reusable container with water instead of buying bottled water. Then donate the money you save to an agency that will help build safe water resources for those with no access. A very small change, a simple sacrifice on our part, would mean a huge difference across the world.

> **"For I will pour water on the thirsty land, and streams on the dry ground."**
>
> *Isaiah 44:3*

When you know better . . .

4,200 children will die today from water-related illness.

. . . You do better

Unless it is an emergency, stop buying the expensive and needless in the form of bottled water. Instead, help H_2O for Life dig and build another well for those with no water.

Precious Cargo?

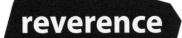 **reverence** — gratitude amplified by recognition of source

 **entitlement** — our failure to have taught the concept of reverence

 **live locally** — one possible reaction to a sense of entitlement and realization of our systemic interconnectedness

 **orange** — a warm color and warm feeling

I n our family, we didn't put out Christmas stockings for Santa to fill at the holidays. Our tradition was to open most of the gifts (notice the plural) on Christmas Eve and then, lo and behold, on Christmas morning, one big gift was under the tree from Santa.

As we grew up, I remember hearing about Christmas way back when and the gifts of seasons past. My mom told us, with a kind of pride laced with nostalgia, of Christmases she experienced. Back then, one of the best presents was, of all things, an orange. Oranges, back then, were a precious cargo crated in a wooden box with some ornately drawn labels pasted to the end. Each orange was individually wrapped in the softest of papers and placed into a nook or chamber of a cardboard insert which was nestled into the box with the rest of this special cargo.

They received this orange in a stocking filled with a few other treasures that came only on very special occasions. I remember seeing these crates of fruit in my younger years at my great-grandparents' grocery store on Broadway Street in Menomonie, Wisconsin. Ole and Inga (no, I'm not kidding) owned and ran the store, and I remember our trips into the store as fun and laced with a little anticipation, as they had an ice cream counter and we, the great-grandkids, always got a cone. I recall that there were only a couple of flavor choices, nothing like what exists today. Certainly there were no toppings or mixings to request.

What that orange represented is, for the most part, gone in today's world. We now have access virtually to any kind of fruit, vegetable, spice, meat, and so forth at any time of the year. Giant big-box supermarkets and gourmet grocery stores carry everything and anything. An orange in the Midwest in December is no more special today than is a mango in Alaska in January. All can be had for a price, but at what price ultimately?

Where does the food I consume come from? How are others affected by my food choices?

The new reality of being able to get whatever we want whenever we want it has moved us into a society that knows no limitation of want. Now, everywhere, we are told that to have a balanced diet we need to eat foods in the winter months of non-production here in the Midwest that are only growing halfway around the world. We don't think twice about those melons on the grocery shelf in the dead of winter or about where they were grown. I know a fresh fruit salad in midwinter would have been impossible for my mom growing up during the Depression. Now we think nothing of such a salad presented on breakfast buffets filled with bounty from around the world. I wonder if nutrition was really that compromised during those earlier years? I don't recall reading about scurvy in the United States post-WWII.

The monetary costs are obvious, but globally they have an environmental impact of huge proportions. To have plump strawberries off-season is a question of resource allocation. The resources

necessary to grow them, pick them, and ultimately to transport them are huge. True respect for resources would mean much more local consumption and a kind of forced seasonal existence that my generation really does not know about. It would require a mindset change that an entitled generation may not be willing to make. At the very least, this means spending our money on organic, additive free, and fair trade produce and products, not pesticide laden cheap goods.

Our global nature of life means a diversity of experience that has exploded across many fronts. We can see instantly across the world, can experience it through music, art, food, literature. As a result, we are much more connected across the planet—or are we? Has knowing that almost three billion people in the world live on less than two dollars a day changed how we look at allocation of resources? Has the universality of our world opened our eyes to view ways to help each other? Or has it meant we want more of what is not a normal part of our world where we live?

What does that orange in the dead of winter represent? Is it the gold of a limited resource shared for a short period of time and savored because of its rarity and beauty? Is it a symbol of an insatiable appetite for more and more no matter what the cost? If that orange represented a fair wage for the grower, picker, and trucker based on fuel efficiency and environmental respect—would we pay the real price of this piece of gold? Perhaps researching where food comes from can help us make good seasonal choices. Don't give up on fresh produce but be a wise consumer.

That carefully picked and packed, transported, and lovingly purchased (maybe at a great sacrifice) orange represents our world and us. Do we take the planet for granted, or is it a precious piece of fruit to be revered and treated with respect and ultimately with profound gratitude?

> **"We have indigestion from overeating, yet let our neighbor starve."**
>
> *Carlo Caretto*

Simple stories . . .

A world gone mad with exploitation of natural resources for insatiable wants.

. . . simple solutions

A return to a predominantly local, agrarian food chain where transport and treatment of products is minimalized. Ultimately, a healthier and more sustainable, simpler form of existence.

Ah, the Simple Egg

 **refusal**   a powerful agent for change

 **ease**   a bill of goods sold to us by clever marketers with little vision for the future mess we would all end up in

 **egg**   pre-packaged by Mother Earth

 **waste**   funny, how as we grow piles of this, so too, have our own midsections expanded

Knowledge is power, but it is also in some ways a curse. If you know more about something, should that knowledge alter your behavior? Is it difficult not to react? Actually, a great deal of our inner mind battling is spent in the justification battleground. This is the area of thought where we justify a behavior even though we "know" it is bad for us or bad for others or bad for the planet. I propose we add another R to our list of Rs or behavioral "shoulds" (REUSE, RECYCLE, REDUCE) and that R is REFUSE.

Recently, my husband and I were on one of those big supermarket excursions, one where you pretty much need something from every category in the store. Up and down all the aisles in our local big-box and low-price supermarket, we came to the dairy aisle and found ourselves standing in front of the eggs. I had decided—here is where the "knowledge" factor comes into play—that we were going to start buying organic eggs. (I had recently seen a segment about regular vs. organic and thought we would definitely make the change to organic eggs). With my husband standing close by, I looked over the selection of eggs. The organic eggs, much to my surprise, were packaged in a Styrofoam (polystyrene) container that was encased in clear plastic. How absurd that an organic egg is sitting in plastic.

Knowing what I know, I very loudly said, "I can't believe that an organic product is put into Styrofoam packing and then wrapped again in more plastic!

I refuse to buy these. How can they put organic eggs in plastic? Now what am I going to do?"

Standing with my husband was an employee of the store. I could hear my husband answer the question that I must not have heard with, "Yes, she is serious. She knows [here we go again with the knowledge] a lot about plastic and she does speak out about it." They laughed as only a couple of guys sharing a joke about a crazy wife can. I wasn't offended; just once again reminded that not everyone knows what everyone else does. What might look like a perfect little cushioned and protected container to protect precious organic eggs is another woman's poison. I refused to buy them. I could not put organic eggs on our table knowing that the packaging—generally not recyclable—would end up in a landfill somewhere. I know too much.

As Americans, we throw away huge amounts (and the estimates vary) of plastic every year. What was once a culture of almost forced recycling has become a culture of pure trash. Soda pop was always in a glass bottle. Now even aluminum cans are rarer, having been replaced by plastic. We think very little of using plastic. It is everywhere. We throw out huge amounts of plastic. It now clogs our planet and our lives.

In the Pacific Ocean a few hundred miles north of Hawaii is a mass of floating plastic called the Great Pacific Garbage Patch. It is about twice the size of the state of Texas and getting bigger

Can we re-examine our lives for possible common sense changes?

all the time. Google it. You'll see the contents. Scientists have studied it for years now and guess what? It is made up of all of our garbage—plastic mostly—and a disgusting mess like you've never seen before.

The problem with plastic—with all trash—is that we don't have to live with it. We "get rid" of it and we throw it away. It magically goes somewhere, and we do not have to see it or deal with it. Out of sight and out of mind.

We think nothing of bringing home grocery bags filled with packaging—not real food. We remove the colorful cardboard box and take out our meal of chicken, rice, and vegetables in a tasty Oriental sauce. We take the meal from the cardboard box and place the plastic tray in the microwave, but not before venting the plastic film over the tray to prevent microwave food blow-up. After a few minutes, we remove the hot tray, stir, and enjoy. The box, the tray, and the plastic film all neatly disposed of in our kitchen trash to be picked up next Wednesday by our trash company on trash day. We never had to peel a carrot, dice a piece of chicken, boil some rice, or even wash a dish.

Growing up in a home where most everything was cooked from scratch, and we grew a great deal of our food, the whole concept did and still does feel strange. Preparing and cooking food was part of being in a family. The time spent together was part of our relationship building.

We have removed ourselves from much of the growing and processing of food (though we sort of cook in the microwave), but we still have to eat. The argument for the convenience foods, as we call them, is that we just don't have the time to cook real food anymore. I don't buy it. We don't take the time and pretty soon, because we don't, no one is going to know how. Soup, it comes in a can. Rice, it comes in a pouch. Salad, it comes in a bag, and the list goes on and on.

Our lack of REFUSAL has led us to this point, but we can change. Let's refuse to be too busy, and let's refuse to use our precious resources to package products, only to throw the packaging away. Refuse! Refuse to buy it or use it if you know something. If you don't know about what you are using, then learn about it.

Our awareness will hopefully lead us to more education. Education compels us to act in different ways. You don't have to buy the organic eggs in Styrofoam wrapped in plastic. Refuse and then find better options. If they don't exist, then demand them by walking away with your most powerful weapons—your pocketbook and your conscience.

> **"It was a chilly, overcast day when the horseman spied the little sparrow lying on its back in the middle of the road. Reining in his mount, he looked down and inquired of the fragile creature, 'Why are you lying upside down like that?' 'I heard the heavens are going to fall today,' replied the bird. The horseman laughed, 'And I suppose your spindly legs can hold up the heavens?' 'One does what one can,' said the little sparrow."**
>
> *Anonymous, from* Peace Moments *compiled by Marlene Bertke, OSB*

What's wrong with this picture?

Island of garbage twice the size of Texas floating in the middle of the northern Pacific Ocean composed of our trash, ranging in depth from a few inches to three hundred feet.

Retake

Absolutely everything is recycled and reused. Nothing is made unless it can be repurposed into something else at the end of its current lifespan. We no longer throw away, we reuse.

Lucy's Coat

thrift — a much maligned form of recycling, perfect for the time we live in—everything old is new again

accumulation — the result of denial or of years of not having to do your own cleaning

Golden Rule — it exists as part of every major religion—why is it not more prevalent in our world?

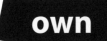
own — a word that should be stricken from our language

My great friend Lucy is among the world's gems. In the later years of her life, she has really perfected the art of thrift-store shopping. This has only happened in her later years because now, in her seventies, she can enjoy some minimal free time. If you look up "multi-tasker" in the dictionary, there will be her picture. I think she has had three or four major careers of which I know—and probably many more minor ones. Now, technically in retirement, she does her age group proud through many volunteer efforts and, of course, some thrift shopping.

Lucy knows the area thrift stores, the days when additional discounts can be had, and keeps a running list of items she is looking for. Along with necessities, she has also picked up Limoges porcelain and hand-painted crystal. What makes this shopping noteworthy is not what treasures may have been found but rather the motivation behind the shopping. Lucy is a living testimony to the life she professes to carry in her soul. That is, that things and appearances truly are the trappings of a shallow life, and what matters most is what you give away. On a very meager living allowance, she manages to honor all her friends and family at special occasions with found and minimally priced treasures. I can honestly say that some of the best gifts I have ever received were ones she lovingly found during her forays into the thrift world. If she can't find it or doesn't have the money for it, she will give it to you, literally, right off her back.

One very cold Minnesota winter day, she was at one of our local charity houses where the homeless and less fortunate go for clothes and living supplies. She was, no doubt, dropping off some found items or things from her own house, and she noticed a woman without a coat. Lucy took off the one she was wearing and gave it to the woman. A remarkable instance in and of itself, made more so knowing she did not have another one waiting in the closet at home. I know she went for a few days without a warm jacket until I heard this story from her housemate and friend Catherine. At this point, I went into my coat closet of way too many choices and brought her a coat. I am not sure how long she would have gone without a proper warm coat, but you see, it didn't really matter to her. She knew at some point another one would show up and decided to just live with it. A couple of years later, she still wears the one that replaced her very warm coat, and I know, if the need presented itself again, Lucy would be coatless.

I wonder what happened to the woman who got Lucy's gift? I wonder if it transformed her in a great way and if she changed her view of this big, cruel world. I wonder if she paid it forward and passed something on to someone else. We will never know. What I do know is that this act of Lucy's solidified in my mind a few truths. We are not defined by our possessions, only our willingness to part with them. Lucy demonstrated the universal principle of give and it will be given to you, poured out in measure for measure. She gave without regard for herself in a true sense of justice.

How willing are we to part with our possessions, our attitudes, our memes?

She literally took the coat off her back. Where there is need, there is where we need to be.

When I see my friend in the coat I gave her to replace the one she so lovingly took off her body, I am often moved to tears. I look away to compose myself, for she would never want recognition for her act of kindness. Her coat reminds me of what we really have things for.

> "The measure of a life will not be in what you accumulate, but in what you give away."
>
> *Wayne Dyer*

How our choices . . .

Lives filled to overflowing with stuff, necessitating ever-expanding places to store the stuff–why do we have separate storage units apart from our homes and the need for bigger closets?

. . . define us.

Essential clothing no longer has to be purchased—it is considered a basic need, provided to all like food or water or the air we breathe. Better yet, where the climate allows it, clothing is totally optional.

Margaret's Thanksgiving Turkey

ingenuity — one resource stretched to many rewards

apathy — an attitude that keeps people in a perpetual state of hunger

Thanksgiving — a practiced-once-a-year holiday that should be our daily practice

leftovers — meant to fill the hunger gap, not the trash

A dear friend is a dear gift. Through our interactions, we are enriched and hopefully challenged to grow into better people. Margaret is a most recently developed friend. We can challenge each other, but in a very loving way. We have known each other for only a few years now and can speak on the phone for what often grows to over an hour as minutes just slip by. I have not known a time with her where either one of us is at a loss for words. With Margaret, I can discuss the passions of my life. She has invariably read an article, seen a program, or heard a statistic to add to whatever topic we are discussing. We challenge each other's thoughts and conclusions and debate points and, in the end, come out with better, broader understandings of the issues of our planet. Our focus in our talks is not on who is right, who is wrong, who knows more, who doesn't, but on how we move forward together and for the good of all. To this end, last December, here's how the conversation went.

We were talking about Thanksgiving, and Margaret mentioned that she had prepared an organic, free-range turkey for dinner. Knowing that she lives on a small budget and hearing her express the expense of this bird, I knew it was a big deal and had potentially made for financial sacrifice in other areas. She spoke about still wanting to eat meat at Thanksgiving. She was also trying to be more responsible both to herself as the consumer of organic meat (pesticide-free, hormone-free, etc.) and to the bird as having lived a more natural life being free-range. Knowing that no set of adjectives to describe a product can ever make it the perfect choice to consume, Margaret chose to sacrifice financially to make a positive impact for her world.

What ensued after Thanksgiving is what I applaud her for. She spoke about the twenty-six meals she and her housemate shared from this one turkey: everything from the original turkey dinner to turkey sandwiches, casserole, tacos, pot pie, and turkey soup. The lesson is one I remember from my childhood, having seen it practiced by folks in my parents' generation. The lesson is that nothing, absolutely nothing, is wasted.

Today, we don't even give table scraps to animals any more because they are "unhealthy." In the sixties, I used to help feed Rusty, my granny and grandpa's dog. We used a can of Vets dog food and the leftovers or, in the worst of cases, some old stale bread mixed in with his food. We now buy designer dog foods, targeted to particular ages and ailments. I wonder if Rusty would like food for mature dogs with dry skin as much as he liked canned Vets with some leftover turkey juices and stale bread. I wish he were alive today to do the test.

Can we see the connection between our clean plates and a hungry person?

Anyway, as our conversation ensued, we started talking about how much food is wasted or thrown away in this country from homes and restaurants and stores. We both agreed it was probably more than we thought, but didn't really know the figures. Well, here they are. In a May 18, 2008, article in the New York Times, as sourced from a federal study, about one hundred billion pounds of edible food (not the spoiled stuff!) was wasted in one year in this country. That amounts to about one pound of food trashed per day per person (for every adult and child in the United States). The photo in this article showed the pile of food thrown out each month for a family of four. The total thrown out for a family of four equaled a staggering 122 pounds.

So, back to the discussion. If we are all culpable and we all waste food, what can we do? Well, as Margaret so amply demonstrated, eat your leftovers. Just because you can afford to throw it out doesn't mean you should. Freeze them, eat them for lunch the next day, give them to someone who will eat them. Plan ahead for meals in the week or you could feed the dog. Invite a friend over if you made too much. Plan better next time. Don't overbuy. Pick up something to donate to a food shelf. Use less and enjoy it more. Donate the money you save to a hunger charity. Help out at a soup kitchen. Show respect for resources and use them wisely.

This same article stated that if we could recover only 5% of the food thrown out, we could feed four million people a day. Please know that, according to World Vision, fourteen thousand children die of hunger every day. With food prices soaring and extreme food shortages looming, an effort to not waste food seems only prudent. Hungry people are not happy people.

Not a month goes by that we don't receive some kind of plea for help for those in the world who are hungry. It's probably because we are on "those lists" and we have given before that we get these mailers begging for help. They come not only from agencies working halfway around the world, but from groups who try to feed the hungry right here in our own state—not even five miles from where we live. What is so sad is that the experts say this is a problem we could solve. No one, absolutely no one, needs to starve or even go to bed hungry.

They say where there is a will there will be a way. Why are we not willing? This is a solvable situation.

I wonder what kind of peace and goodwill and general happiness would pervade this world if only everyone were fed.

"Gather the pieces that are left over, let nothing be wasted"

John 6:12

Common sense . . .

"Thousands of people die every day from hunger, while we in the United States throw out about a pound of edible food per person per day."

... for Common good.

Finally, literally, the scales are balanced. Less food wasted in lands of plenty means more resources freed up for those in need.

Headed Up North

 **speed**   for most of us, the admonition to take time in our busy lives and smell the roses holds more truth than we care to admit

 **family**   motivating factor

 **exhaust**   as in tired or a byproduct of burning up–probably one and the same

 **conservation**   the act of which seems inversely related to stress; think of how slowly we move when it is hot

W e thought long and hard about a trip to my dad's grave this Memorial Day, mostly because of the price of gas. In the seventeen years since he died, at least one of the family (Mom or us kids) have made the two-hour drive to place flowers on his grave. Because he was buried in the Veterans Cemetery of a small Wisconsin town, it is the only time we are allowed to place anything on his grave. Gas was four dollars a gallon in the summer of 2008.

What placed enough weight on the scale to tip it in the favor of taking the trip was the chance to see some of the "rellies" (relatives). My aunt is in a care facility and well into her nineties, and my other aunt and uncle still live in this little town. With thoughts of seeing them and having some time together, my husband and I decided to make the trip.

Part of the trip is on a major freeway through Minnesota, heading north, before you cut over and onto two-lane roads into Wisconsin. What was amazing was that, for most of the trip, on the interstate four-lane freeway with a speed limit of seventy miles per hour, we were being passed as we held our speed to about sixty-five miles per hour—and passed quickly. It was more than obvious to us that those passing were exceeding the speed limit by quite a bit. Recall, gas was then at four dollars per gallon.

Some political pundits were on a talk show I watched recently, asking themselves what it would take for people to slow down or drive less—obviously not the price of gas. Do most people know that driving faster may get you to your destination faster, but that it also burns more fuel? By our experience as we headed north, I don't think so.

Greg Haegele, the director of conservation for the Sierra Club, states that the Union of Concerned Scientists (they care, they really care) say that by decreasing from seventy to sixty miles per hour, you improve fuel efficiency by about 17%. Going from seventy-five to fifty-five improves it by about 30%. In an average family car, for every ten miles per hour you drive over sixty, it is like paying about fifty cents more per gallon of gas you paid for originally at $3.25 per gallon. Let's slow down. They also state that on a three-hundred-mile trip driving at sixty-five, not seventy-five miles per hour, means you get there only twenty minutes later.

Now, factor in the amount of carbon dioxide you are not putting into the air by having to drive fast to get wherever you are going. Slower going can be easier on the nerves, too!

My husband has a saying where he's from: they say, "soon come." That can, in actuality, mean you might see him in ten minutes or an hour, maybe even tomorrow. The promise is not that he will get there at any particular time, just that he will get there. The lesson in "soon come?" Unless somebody's life depends upon your timely arrival, let's learn to loosen up and be a little more like those folks in the rest of the world and "soon come."

> **"As you are, so is the world."**
>
> *Ramana Maharshi*

What value do we place on time? What value does family have?

Pre-paradigm shift . . .

Speed, coupled with
the stress of its added
burdens, creates a
world of always bigger,
better, faster, more and
more, and the values
of time over safety,
conservation, and
environment–
"Go fast."

... Post-paradigm shift.

Speed limits reduced to reflect safety and conservation principles first and foremost and relatives are visited more than once a year as we take more time to stop and smell the roses.

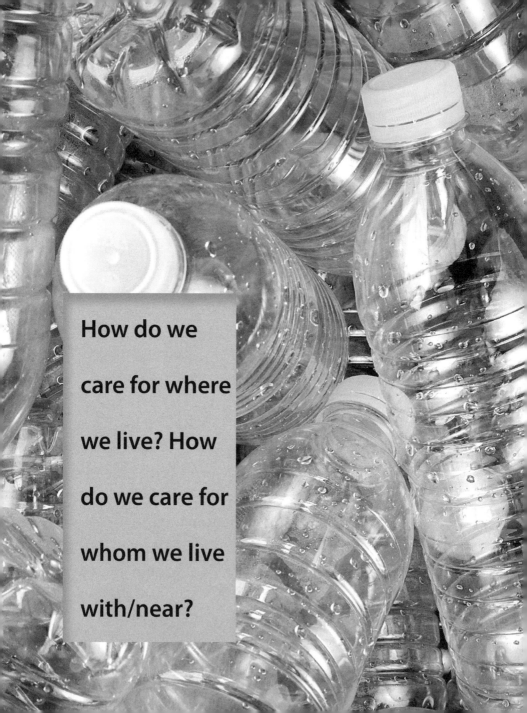

How do we care for where we live? How do we care for whom we live with/near?

Grandpa's House of Stuff

 **clutter** one man's trash is another man's treasure

 **value** some of us keep everything, hoping for this some day; some of us get rid of it all, knowing reality

 **repurpose** as your inventiveness expands, so too does this potential

 **pie** funny how, at the end of life, it all comes down to this

M y grandfather was the ultimate saver. He saved everything. He saved plastic milk jugs, aluminum pie tins, plastic pie-tin covers (he ate a lot of pie and drank a lot of milk), newspapers, dog-food bags, plastic takeout containers, bread bags, twisties, rubber bands, cardboard boxes—well, you get the picture. He cleaned all of these things up and then placed them neatly in piles around the house. When he ran out of places to make piles, he rigged up string and hung up some things— like the milk jugs. The problem was, he collected it all, and collected more and then more, but it never went anywhere, except to some place in his home.

He lived in a small Wisconsin town long before the curbside recycling pickup we have today. There was no one in the eighties who coordinated the pickup of all the various types of recycling. You could say he was ahead of his time in knowing that he should save these items. He lacked the follow-through to get them to all of their various recycling destinations, many as they were at that time in our history.

Thank goodness, it is so much easier now. There really is not a viable excuse these days not to recycle. I wish we had more public recycling bins available as they do in other countries. The easier it is, the more likely we are to do it. Most municipalities provide curbside bins (sometimes free of charge), and you simply set out your recycling along with trash on pickup day. Only a few of our plastics are recyclable now, and we do need to work to change this because many fossil fuels are simply being wasted as plastics are manufactured in record amounts.

When my granny was alive, the house was never so laden with piles of recycling. I wonder if she threw out those items or was just more efficient in getting them where they needed to go. She also baked a whole lot more of those pies from scratch, so a bought pie was not a part of their lives when she was around. When she passed, many years before my grandfather, we also did not purchase so much prepared food and hence there was less packaging to get rid of. As grandfather aged, he bought more and more packaged, prepared food, especially pies. I remember seeing two, sometimes three, pies in the refrigerator along with a gallon or two of milk when we visited him in the years just before he passed. He loved pie. My mom would "put up" meals for him. Sometimes we brought over whole coolers full of food to place in his deep freeze for his dinners.

It is funny how his generation's penchant for saving everything has morphed into our generation's penchant for throwing out everything. What was different about his generation and my father's generation and how they grew up? Obviously, a different sense of what was worth something and what was trash.

I think Grandpa would have been the neighborhood green guy. His recycling bins would have been curbside every Wednesday along with the small bag of trash unable to be recycled.

Now it all comes back to me. I know why they tried to accumulate so little trash. Because whatever you threw out meant a trip to the dump. You hauled it yourself; no curbside pickup like today. No wonder they tried so hard not to throw out stuff. Maybe we have become callous to what we throw out because we don't have to deal with it. It disappears from our trash bins on Wednesday, like magic, but where is all our trash? More importantly, what is it doing to the planet?

I applaud my grandfather's efforts, regardless of whether he was an environmentalist ahead of his time or just trying to avoid a trip to the dump. He had the right idea; he tried not to trash the world.

> **If we do not change our direction, we are likely to end up where we are headed."**
>
> *Ancient Chinese Proverb*

Piles and piles and piles . . .

The clutter and trash of our lives have taken over the planet. Shouldn't the piles have some purpose beyond just being a pile? How can we be so stupid as to make more and more piles and suffocate ourselves?

. . . transformed to alter our lives.

Everything has a use and everything is utilized. Very little is thrown away, and we live a life of uncluttered simplicity–free to think and move as we once did with the planet–all breathing as one.

How have you sown for future generations?

Dad's Trees

 **sow** planting, as in a tree, a seed, an idea

 **mindless** going through life with the notion that not everything one chooses to do matters to anyone or anything but self

 **tree** a symbol of our willingness to be mindful

 **reap** the biblical and agricultural equivalent of "what goes around, comes around," or indisputable proof for paying it forward

O n the highway between Siren and Spooner, Wisconsin, a few miles west of Spooner, is a huge stand of pine trees that are between eighty and a hundred feet tall. They were planted by my dad some fifty-odd years ago as a favor to a friend. Nothing has ever been built on this piece of land, and the pines stand as a stronghold to the earth beneath them. It's probably a miracle that so many of the seedlings, no more than a few inches in height when planted, survived without subsequent watering and attention. They were planted and then left to Mother Nature to tend.

My dad was no great conservationist. He did enjoy the outdoors and loved to garden and fish. I'm not sure what his thoughts would be about global climate change, but I do know he loved this part of Wisconsin—"God's country" he called it. I would like to think he would have a set of reusable bags in the trunk for trips to the grocery store. Save a tree, you know. I am amazed how many folks still use the bags, be they paper or plastic, that the store provides. It is so easy to have a few of your own reusable bags these days. Most stores sell them for a dollar or two, and they have so many uses beyond just toting groceries home from the store. I use them whenever and wherever I shop now, taking them into the drugstore, hardware store, grocery, and big-box store, anywhere I know I might need a bag. Surprisingly, it hasn't totally caught on yet. In Europe, this is all you see. Everyone has their own bags to pack up whatever they purchase. This practice saves on resources, saves on trash, and saves on trees.

If we think more carefully about what we purchase and how we transport it, there are many more possibilities for our conversation than you might think. We have all been told that we should take a multivitamin for our health because very few of us eat all of the recommended servings of our fruits and veggies, nor do we get certain important vitamins and nutrients in the average American diet. There's a vitamin company right here in America that produces its products using only solar power. All of the company's production is solar-based. I buy these vitamins because they do me good and because they are responsible to the environment. I call it a win-win!

Another company I purchase from uses 80-90% recycled products and powers their production with wind power. They also pay living wages to indigenous peoples who provide the raw materials for their products. If you look, you can make these choices and support a sustainable environment. More and more opportunity exists to do this every day, and companies are now telling us they are conservationists because it helps to sell their products.

I've planted a few trees in my life, but not anywhere near what my dad did. I am going to make an effort to do more. Everywhere around us, as more and more buildings go up and concrete goes down, we lose the face of Mother Earth. It is up to us to make sure she remains beautiful. Use a green product, fill only your own reusable bags, opt for less packaging, and plant a tree or two or three. Years from now, folks will see the fruit of your labors and Mother Earth's face will smile.

As a former science teacher, when I taught kids and then later trained teachers to teach science, I used to tell them that there were some basic facts and theories that everyone on this planet should know. One of those is that many plants take in carbon dioxide and give off oxygen. As we destroy the rain forests and spew carbon dioxide into the atmosphere by burning fossil fuels, this fact becomes even more important. If you are somehow responsible for removing plants or trees from this planet, by for instance, your use of paper or clearing of land, then replace those trees. Our very existence is predicated on our understanding of this basic scientific fact. Plants take in carbon dioxide and give off oxygen. It could be no simpler. It could be no more direct. Plant a tree … breathe.

> **"I am only one, but still I am one. I cannot do everything, but still I can do something, and because I cannot do everything, I will not refuse to do the something that I can do."**
>
> *Edward Everett Hale*

Our world looks like this . . .

Massive systemic destruction of whole ecosystems based on a disregard for basic principles of life-sustaining practice. No more trees. More parking.

. . . or this?

Preserved for all time and all future generations, a planet that supports itself and sustains life.

The Big Lake

respect
the under-everything, framework feeling that connects us for all time

loss
tragically associated with the notion of "gone for all time"

original
never again to be reproduced in the same way—as in our planet

Gitchee Gumee
the big lake, they called it this and revered it for its power and mystery

Imagine all of North America and South America covered by one foot of water. Now take all that water and pour it into one great big giant bowl. That bowl would be a vessel we now call Lake Superior. The world's largest body of freshwater, this great lake contains three quadrillion gallons of water.

On a recent trip up to the North Shore of Minnesota, we stayed at a place located right along the water's edge. Lake Superior is known for being a lake of many moods, many faces. On the first day of our trip, as we sat on a piece of driftwood cast upon the shore, the lake was so quiet and calm as to be almost eerie. We spoke to each other in hushed tones and could hear each other perfectly. When a flock of six or seven Canada geese flew overhead, it was so quiet we could hear their wings beating with the rush of air under these birds.

The next day in the afternoon, the lake was churning up whitecaps and the waves crashed along the rocky shore. The sound was so intense that my husband could not hear me call to him. He was no more than fifty feet away.

The basaltic rocks of this shore made it difficult to move quickly, and every step resulted in a shifting of these rocks under our feet. For as far as the eye could see, there was nothing but water—three quadrillion gallons of it.

About 250 feet away and inside the nice warm lounge of this resort was a huge aquarium of freshwater fishes from this lake. We sat at a table with a nose-to-nose view of the inhabitants of this tank. Literally, only a pane of glass separated me from these fish and their watery world. I sat quite mesmerized, eyeball to eyeball, with what I think I remembered as a perch.

Even while diving, I have never been that close to a living fish, able to see even the smallest of detail. This living creature came into full-blown, high-definition color, every external aspect viewed by me for the first time, at least at this level. The colors were not even close to the rainbow assortment of fish in the Caribbean, but there was a grand elegance to the combination of golds, greens, and browns in this exquisite little animal.

I was most fascinated by the movement of its pectoral fin. I had never seen a fish move a fin in this manner while remaining almost motionless in terms of changing position. The pectoral fin rotated, swayed, and moved in a domino effect as the fish remained fixed in one spot. It reminded me of an old amusement park ride we loved as kids called the Tilt-o-Whirl. While rotating in a large circle, your capsule could also rotate both clockwise and counterclockwise and meander up and down over small bumps on the path.

And, it wasn't the liquor talking. I had only had half a Bloody Mary. It was truly the wonderment of nature. I don't know if this pectoral fin movement is unique to this species of fish or not. I was drawn to the complexity of this fish and being able to see it in an almost voyeuristic fashion. My college biology major had never seemed so real to me as in this moment of contact with this one fish.

How do we treat the life of our Earth?

To imagine what is in that great lake of three quadrillion gallons of water is mind-blowing. Think of the detail inscribed as part of every living thing inhabiting that lake. Think of the breadth and depth of the type of animals and plants in that one lake and then multiply that times all of the unique habitats in the world. Such biodiversity is astounding.

Conservationists now say that one out of every four mammals on this planet is in danger of extinction. One out of every two populations of mammals is in decline. Can we shrink our own footprints on the planet to make room for theirs?

One such mammal is the polar bear. I recall reading about the individual strands of a polar bear's fur. They are actually clear and hollow. The bear appears white because of an undercoat of fur close to the skin, but these fur strands that stick up are colorless. They are the only bear on this planet that has fur strands like this, and these animals are now in danger of extinction—real, documented danger.

Whether it is from global climate change, or whatever reason you want to attribute it to, isn't it an ultimate tragedy that one in four mammals face this level of permanent destruction? If the polar bear dies out as a species, what we have lost is probably only a section of a brush stroke that is on the canvas we call Earth. The tragedy is in not knowing what piece of the painting is gone. And isn't the whole work of art, our planet, diminished by damage to a small spot? How many spots can be damaged before the canvas no longer resembles the original and has lost its value?

At our local city zoo, a polar bear makes his habitual circle around a path worn deep into concrete by his giant padded feet. When we visit the zoo, there are always a handful of kids with their noses pressed up against the glass of his swimming pool in a futile attempt to get even closer to the giant. I am sure that, given half a chance, they would venture into the frigid water and swim with the bear.

I know the feeling. For me, it was a Lake Superior perch that mesmerized my imagination and moved me out of my human skin, if only for a bit. To watch that fish that closely was to be a part of it if only in my mind and if only for a few minutes.

The polar bear at our zoo is gone now. Off staying at another zoo while they reconstruct his digs. He will have a bigger and more "polar-bearish" place to live, and we will all be able to see him again very soon. Or will we?

> "Probably every generation sees itself as charged with remaking the world. Mine, however, knows it will not remake the world. Its task is even greater: to keep the world from destroying itself."
>
> *Albert Camus*

Extinction is permanent . . .

About one species becomes extinct every twenty minutes, and the polar bear will be gone by the end of this century.

Respect is eternal . . .

All kids, for all time, will be able to know of all of nature, not just the nature that has survived us.

What On Earth Is a Chiton?

progress — a euphemism for "build it and they will come," a.k.a. greed

insatiable — the appetite has many faces, why haven't we learned to control it?

restraint — in the face of temptation, it will always, always lead to no regrets the morning after

chiton — simple symbol of world gone mad

There is an incredibly beautiful spot on Earth that I have had the privilege to visit for some twenty-eight years, mostly yearly, sometimes more than once a year. The first time I went there, it was for a marine biology interim class, and I studied chitons. Chitons are small, eight-plated invertebrates that inhabit mainly the intertidal zones of shore areas. I had found quite a few of them in an area called Eden Rock on some rocky shore and decided they would be my subjects while on the island.

Back in the early eighties, the Cayman Islands were relatively unknown. Situated south of Cuba and west of Jamaica, they were kind of like a small town in Wisconsin. If you blink while passing through, you might miss it. Large stretches of relatively unspoiled shore still existed, and you could walk for great distances, miles even, on pristine white sand beach. Holiday Inn was "the" spot on Seven-Mile Beach, and you could enjoy a hamburger at the McDonald's in town. Be prepared for at least a twenty-minute wait; however, the lounge attached next door was a good place to pass the time.

Ah, those were the days. That was then and this is now. Why is that phrase so true for so many places? Back in the eighties, there was some kind of building regulation which prohibited anything over three stories going up along the stretch of Seven-Mile Beach. I remember hearing something like that they never wanted the buildings to tower over the beautiful pines that swayed in the tropical breezes.

Fast forward to today. Seven-Mile Beach is a conglomeration of multistory hotels and condos aimed at those with lots of money and not much sense. The regulation is gone. The excessive building has lead to an exhausting array of bigger and more elaborate buildings, all competing for space with each other. It reminds me of crabs in a barrel, all piling up on one another in an effort to claw their way to the top for a look at the prize. The problem is that, once out of the barrel, the prize so coveted has now disappeared.

This once-beautiful stretch of beach, rivaled by none that I have ever seen, looks now like every other stretch of beach in every other previously undeveloped tropical paradise. The view is gone and the peace has been destroyed.

Hopefully the government and the people of the Cayman Islands will put aside some important lands now, lands that cannot ever be touched. Future generations will thank them for preserving what once was the most important part of this island, its natural beauty, not its ability to generate cash. Maybe we need to think about what kind of economic and environmental attitude we are supporting with our vacation dollars.

Those chitons I studied are no longer at Eden Rock. The place where I studied them, guess what, has been developed. I hope they found another safe place somewhere nearby and that they are hanging on for dear life.

How do we measure real progress?

"People who will not sustain trees will soon live in a world which cannot sustain people."

Bryce Nelson

What is wrong with this picture?

Loss of everything that truly defines paradise: unspoiled natural resources. Too many hotels and condos with too many of the same names–only different locations.

What is right with this picture?

The preservation and redefinition of paradise based upon natural beauty. We come to visit the environment, not to live in an artificially created one.

Science for All of Us

reform — when it requires a shift in consciousness, probably very difficult, but not impossible to achieve

literacy — a scary term for what many people consider a scary subject

vision — needed to move us past where we are headed

2061 — the next year we will see Halley's Comet. Hopefully, I will be alive to view it

H ere in the frozen Midwest, springtime inevitably means news stories about 2 ton trucks having gone throught the ice on some lake. Obviously, this truck belonged to a student who did not pay attention during classes on the temperature at which water freezes and ice formation. Understanding basic science has its merits for a life lived with fewer mishaps. There is some basic science we all need to know.

While a graduate student, I had the opportunity to work on a national project aimed at bettering the state of science education in this country. Project 2061 of the American Association for the Advancement of Science was begun in the early eighties as a huge effort to bolster science education in the United States. The panel, which examined the strand section technology, was located here in Minneapolis-St. Paul, Minnesota.

The chair of our technology panel was as gentle a man as you might ever meet. Under that gentle and so-kind exterior was a brilliant and sometimes ferocious advocate for our science education reform. Jim Johnson, a retired 3M

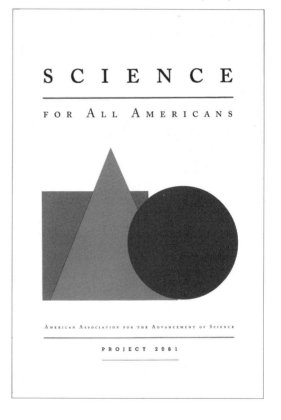

executive scientist, chaired our panel of experts as we met in daylong sessions over about a year with the goal to determine what every American needed to know about technology. We were strongly committed to making a difference in science education in this country. Other focus groups in science and math were scattered across the nation and given the same task, to answer this question: To be a literate population in science, what do high-school graduates need to know about science? The resulting 272-page book called *Science for All Americans* was the final product reflective of huge amounts of time, energy, and expertise by the most brilliant minds in our country.

Why is science so unimportant to our overall education goals? Why do we have such fear of the subject? Fast-forward to 2010. Here we sit with our public schools in the worst shape they have ever been. The budgets for science research have been slashed, and we exist still as a nation addicted to oil—and foreign oil at that. We rank twenty-first out of twenty-one developed countries in science, and a staggering 93% of middle school science teachers have little or no training in science.

I share this because at the time I became involved in Project 2061—back in the early eighties, recall—I felt a real sense of urgency about the state of science education. For all the

How can education help us relate to each other?

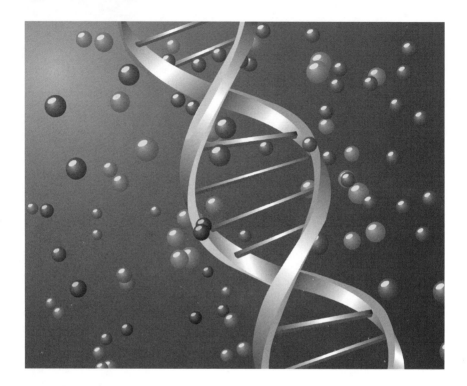

programs and grants and training and projects that have come and gone since then, nothing seems to have changed. No, it has changed. Our rankings have become worse.

I remember, one meeting, joking with one of the scientists who was a regular part of our technology panel, that this book we were working on should be required reading for all high-school graduates. Perhaps now it should be required reading for all science teachers first. How have we reached a place where mediocrity, not excellence, is the expectation and the norm in our students as well as our teachers?

I am sure that a multitude of educational mistakes, missteps, and probably downright sins can explain the mess we are in. But how to get out of it? Probably nothing short of revolution will change the system; for as long as we are willing to look the other way and not take personal responsibility for all of our children, nothing will change. We have tried, but obviously not hard enough, and we are getting further and further behind in a subject critical to our planetary survival.

If Jim were around today, he would probably give a gentle laugh to our current science situation news and then get right down to work–serious and purposeful work. How are we going to move ahead and solve this educational crisis unless we make it a national priority? When will it be a priority? Unless science becomes a mandatory subject for all grades K-12, we will continue to rank at the bottom of lists and solutions to world problems. Twenty-first out of twenty-one is as close to the bottom as you can get.

"When nothing seems to help, I go look at a stonecutter hammering away at a rock perhaps a hundred times without as much as a crack showing in it. Yet at the hundredth and first blow it will split in two and I knew it was not that blow that did it but all that had gone before."

Jacob Riis

World of ignorance

Doomed to a world of ever-increasing problems as we argue about what scientists know as facts because we know not how science really works to explain our world. We burn up before we are all convinced that the science is real.

World of understanding

When presented with
fact, we get right
to work to remedy
problematic human
course and we take
responsibility for our
actions and for what
real science explains.
We slow or even stop
the burn.

A Small Room in the Basement

bounty — so expected in most of our lives that our becoming accustomed to it has hardened our hearts

conservation — the product of a mindset based upon gratitude

squander — what we do as we lose sight of need vs. want

glass jar — a gleaming symbol of a world respected and cherished for its gifts of survival

Fall conjures up many memories. The end of summer and the beginning of a new school year in our house was always punctuated by an additional season—canning. From the first of August to the first frost, our family kitchen was a production site of sometimes-massive efforts to can the summer's bounty before another cold and long winter set in.

At its peak, my father's garden contained peppers, squash, cucumbers, onions, potatoes, beets, and many more kinds of vegetables. His garden always, always, had tomatoes, as I would say, up the ying-yang. In a small typical suburban backyard, there were often fifty or even sixty plants. He didn't use harmful sprays or chemical additives, and these tomatoes were the best I have ever tasted. They were the kind that you just pick ripe from the vine and stand right there, chest-deep in a patch of plants, and eat. With the juices running down your chin, it was the best snack on Earth. I have a photo of my niece at about three years old doing just this. She is dwarfed by the plants in the photo and just sneaking into the shot is my dad's old, weathered hand.

Our garage, in the summers, did not house a car. The floor was filled with boxes of tomatoes at various stages of ripeness, awaiting a canning day. When the tomatoes determined this, we went into action. Jars and lids sterilized, laid out neatly on the terry towels, awaiting their roles. They were poised and ready to be drafted into service.

The process was simple and tedious, yet it afforded whoever was involved a time to connect. I know both my mom and dad canned in solitary silence in that kitchen, but when we worked at it together there was the obvious produce product, but also a shared time I now look back on fondly.

Boiling water to loosen the skin was the first step for the tomato. It only remained in the water for a few-second bath and then was quickly transferred to an ice-water-filled sink to stop the potential cooking and mushing of the fruit.

This whole process is a lot like the Nordic winter custom of sauna, a steamy respite followed by a sprint to the lake and a quick dip into the icy waters. My parents being of Scandinavian descent, this whole process is ironic somehow—mmmm.

Once the tomato had cooled a bit, a nimble slip of the paring knife and off the skin would come. These slippery whole beauties were then placed—not packed I was reminded—into the pristine sterilized quart jars. The filled jars were carefully wiped clean at the rim and ring area, and then the two-part lid was removed from boiling water and placed atop the jar of red summer goodness. After a boiling bath, the jars were carefully removed from the water and placed to cool on terry towels covering the kitchen table. We waited to hear the "ping" from each jar, assuming that the seal had been made manifest and the process complete. Those jars that didn't seal? Well, they were stored in the fridge to become chili or spaghetti in the next few days.

After some admiration time, all of the jars of summer bounty—tomatoes, chow-chow, beets, corn, pickles— were taken downstairs to the basement and the back room. This dark, very cool location in our home always housed the canning. You had to open a door that wouldn't quite open all the way and reach around the corner to pull a light switch cord to see this room's contents, sometimes finding your way in winter in total darkness. The single bulb in this little room revealed shelf upon shelf of gleaming jars filled with the bounty of a backyard

The values we share, where do they come from?

garden. At its peak, the room was filled to overflowing. A tribute to the tremendous yield of a well-tended garden and a penchant not to waste a thing. Talk about eating locally!

The process from planting to canning was not a difficult one. It took time and some generational wisdom, a modicum of physical effort, but not much else besides a place to plant and a will to preserve. I don't know many folks that still can, at least not on the same level that I experienced when growing up. That kind of backyard growing and harvesting has been replaced by farmers'-market shopping and big-box grocers. What we have lost is a real connection to the land and where things come from, the work it takes to grow and harvest food and how we need to treat it.

To demonstrate how we have changed, here is a recent experience. My husband and I were at one of those chain gas stations filling up the gas tank, and as he pumped the gas, I went inside to pay the bill. I witnessed something happening across the store as I stood at the register. A young woman was emptying the baked goods from the shelves into a trash barrel. She took out tray after almost-filled tray and dumped the contents into the barrel. An older woman customer asked her what she was doing. She replied that she did this every night about this same time. She asked what happened to the product, and the girl said she threw it into the garbage. Why? How can food be treated so callously? How can the products of our farms be thrown away? How can the bounty of the Earth be wasted?

The solutions are so painfully obvious they seem ridiculous to mention. Give it to a shelter, put a sign by it that says "free," recycle it to a pig farmer, ask a church if they need free treats—the list is endless. How can we just throw it all away?

In the bleak and dark days of winter, when the sun sets around 4:30 in the afternoon, sometimes I remember a very simple supper in our home of warmed canned tomatoes, a little salt and pepper, maybe a piece of butter and some bread. Boy, you could just about taste summer. I know that these dinners were not had because there was nothing else to eat. These meals were just a part of the enjoyment of planting a plant, getting a product, and tasting the fruits of your labor. Maybe also, that simple food is also very good food.

The reverence for a tomato. I learned this growing up. How 'bout the reverence for a doughnut? That doughnut started somewhere as a plant on this great Earth and probably passed through many hands, some weathered, some old, before it was tossed out with the trash. I wonder what the simple gift of a not-too-much-past-its-prime pastry might have done to help someone's life. We'll never know if we keep throwing 'em in the trash—the doughnuts I mean.

"Nothing could be worse than the fear that one has given up too soon and left one effort unexpended which might have saved the world."
Jane Addams

The simple things . . .

Unbalanced planet of overconsumption and waste which leads to a profound sense of haves and have-nots made manifest by the millions who will die this year of starvation: eight children per minute.
(UNICEF)

. . . are the best.

Reverence for resources, human and Earth, has transformed our planet into one where no one lacks access to food, water, and basic sanitation. The table is finally set and everyone sits at it.

Wisdom For the Ages

togetherness
that awful and much-anticipated aspect of family life that we all crave

life
when mixed with love, a recipe for peace

1937
funny how much it is just like today–well, maybe not so funny

dinner
the daily constancy and sometimes our only place and time to connect with what connects us all

Back in the seventies, as a ninth-grader, I was in my first formal theatrical production. By formal, I mean a real script with costumes, greasepaint, programs, a curtain call, and a two-day run. The show was Moss & Hart's *You Can't Take It with You,* and I had a very minor role as the Grand Duchess Olga Katrina, who appeared on stage at the very end of the show, an afterthought kind of role–at least so I thought.

The Grand Duchess wore a costume of way-past-their-prime clothes from a past life of aristocracy. She had obviously been someone with money and a status at one time in her life, but now she, wearing the remnants of that former life, was a part of a family with no such means. Olga had been taken in by this wacky family as one of their own. No better, no worse because of her lineage or external trappings of a life gone by. She was just an accepted part of the whole family.

The remarkable aspect of this theatrical experience was couched not in the drama of the play, but rather that, as a group of fourteen- and fifteen-year-olds, we were charged with delivering such a message. In the midst of raging hormones, budding teenager experiences, and an abject disregard for anything global in focus, we acted out a message for all time. A message I painfully relearned as an adult.

This play, written in 1937, is as much about today as it was about the today when it was written. We all come into this world with nothing and to the best evidence of our human experience thus far, over time, we leave with nothing. The experiences of life are not tied to stuff, but to exactly that experience. So why, after all this time, are we still so concerned with the state of our lives? We look forward to our futures, not so much concerned about those who will follow us, but about ourselves and how we will live and be taken care of in our old age.

Moss & Hart's comic portrayal of a multigenerational and dysfunctional family living and loving together in what can be called crowded, personal, and privacy-lacking space tells the tale of our world today. Our challenge is to learn to live together and love unconditionally. Maybe this lesson wasn't delivered by the wrong actors—a group of crazy, mixed-up kids with a lifetime to work it all out and learn what is most important in life: You can't take it with you.

> "We haven't got too much time, you know—any of us."
> From *You Can't Take It with You*
>
> *Grandpa*

What is it that we crave in being together?

Where there is no real love . . .

As we separate and define ourselves and our spaces, we continue to fight over resources and leave members of our global family out. When we do not love, there is no peace–of mind or heart or spirit.

... there is no real peace.

No matter what defines our differences, peace becomes the worldwide norm as nothing ever surpasses our connectedness as one human family. As I am with my neighbor, I am with myself, and all I want is peace.

Conclusion

E very real-life example shows within a situation something about who we are. Some of these stories have shown us who we want to be, others who we do not want to be. Ultimately, in each of the stories, there was a time, a moment, or at least a pause where somebody made a choice that defined them and a future. The world is shaped and reshaped daily by all the choices we make. We can continue to live as we have, and we can then pretty much expect to get more of what we are currently living. Our future is the future of our actions today.

Take only one of the themes, for example: world hunger. For years, the experts have told us that we have the means to end this. Let us once and for all do it! And, it might be as simple as not throwing out food. By literally adding up the collective consciousness that allows us to preserve resources and not throw them away, we could feed millions.

Complications, of course, would crowd the ultimate solution to this problem. Maybe we need to stop making excuses tied to potential complications and try.

Compiling evidence of the world views of our today and hopes for our potential tomorrow paints for us a very vivid picture of our current chosen lives and the possibilities for our future. There is alternately astonishing danger and amazing redemption lurking in our futures. In summary, together we can continue in a world of inequalities where needs are met on the basis of a falsely perceived worth, where the planet becomes a trash heap of our inability to recognize excess, where basic survival needs are bought and sold for profit, where starvation is never eliminated, where precious resources are used to support lives of laziness, where "mine is mine is mine and I want more" is our mantra, where we never clean our plates, where we use up all fossil fuels and the planet burns up, where toxicity measures become the norm and bad health increases, where the rain forests are gone, where there is no clean water . . . no, there is no water, where we live in a concrete jungle, where no one understands how we got into this mess let alone how to get out of it, where we have totally lost a connection to Earth and life-support, and where we still believe that having money and property equates with happiness. Together, these chosen beliefs and their resulting actions paint a future that I can't believe we wish to live in.

So, would giving some stuff away, turning off the faucet, learning some more science, not stuffing your face, growing a tomato, spending time with family, scaling down our homes, driving slower, using real silverware, buying only products that can be recycled, planting a tree, or seeing a real polar bear make any difference in our world at all? Fundamentally, this is a question that no one has any real answer for. We don't know for absolutely sure if any or all of these efforts might shift the tidal wave of destruction we seem to be riding on now. What I think we all do know is that we do not want to continue on the path we are on now. We know where we are going to end up.

It is that true, it is that profound, and it is that simple.

> **"Ordinary people with commitment can make an extraordinary impact on their world."**
>
> *John Maxwell*

TODAY . . .

- hunger
- a convenience-based existence
- children die
- insatiable wants
- an island of garbage
- lives overflowing with stuff
- we throw out food
- mantra is "go fast"

- surrounded by suffocating piles
- systemic destruction of ecosystems
- species lost forever
- loss of paradise
- we burn up
- a wasteful planet
- we fight over resources

Some Day . . .

- no one is hungry
- zero waste
- we dig and build wells
- we live a simpler form of existence
- everything is recycled and reused
- all basic needs provided
- scales are balanced
- safety and conservation principles first
- uncluttered simplicity

• a planet that
supports itself
• all people know nature
• reverence for and
respect of
natural beauty
• we stop the burn
• no one lacks access to
food, water, and
basic sanitation
• peace becomes the
worldwide norm

Epilogue

started writing this book about five years ago. In the midst of writing, we have been plunged into yet another major period of re-examination. "They" have named this period of angst we find ourselves in now and they call it the "Great Recession." No one really knows how long this period will last and what we will look like on the back end of it.

Ordinary, decent, hardworking folks have lost their jobs and can't find new ones. They are "underwater" in their houses, owing more than the house is worth, with no real hope of recouping their losses. We are collectively looking at a retirement very different than the one imagined by the value of a 401(k) of a few years back. All of this, juxtaposed with the first three-quarters of 2009 showing that Wall Street had made more than two and a half times more profit than in any other previously recorded time period in history. Two questions come to mind. Why do the ordinary, hardworking, decent folk always seem to draw the short straw, and why are we always talking about money?

Actually, there's a third question. Why are we continually asking these same questions over and over again?

A lot of time has passed since I was an undergraduate, going to college in a small town. A lot has changed, but so much remains the same. While in college, a good friend, Jen, gave me a copy of Shel Silverstein's book *The Giving Tree*. This is a short and poignant children's book, although on the inside flap it says it is "for all ages."

This book tells the story of a boy and a tree and the relationship they share as the boy ages. The tree is always there for him, always giving, even when there is not much to give. The boy goes about life searching for happiness outside of their relationship in things and money. At every step of the journey, the tree does her level best to provide what the boy thinks he needs to achieve happiness. The tree is sad when he goes away to pursue his life without her and is once again happy when the boy returns to ask for more.

As a nation, as a world, we play the role of the boy. We continue to look for happiness outside ourselves, and we focus on money and stuff as the vehicles to this end. Some thirty years after I received my copy of this book, the message written back in the sixties has never been more true. This crisis we are in today in 2010 is not about money, it is not about things, houses, or retirement plans. It is fundamentally about how we treat each other, our relationships, and our willingness to give.

The boy is willing, all the way into old age, to take what he has been taught to believe will make him happy. Without regard for herself, the tree provides all she has, hoping beyond hope for the boy's happiness only to have the boy realize that what she has provided never made him happy. His happiness was and is found in their relationship. Their relationship was all that ever mattered, and the things of life are just that—things. And, it took almost total destruction of his beloved friend, the tree, before he figured it out.

So what is the key to happiness? The wisdom to answer this question is as old as time itself and the sayings we all grew up with. Don't let hate and lack of forgiveness make a place in your heart for "what goes around, comes around." The energy drainers of "worry and stress are just today's mouse eating tomorrow's cheese." "Living simply will allow others to simply live" so "don't put your hat where you cannot reach it." And lastly, "as you sow, so shall you reap."

The great wisdom, whether it be folk wisdom, philosophical wisdom, or biblical wisdom, has always been that: great wisdom.

The key to happiness? Embracing this wisdom and living a life of common sense for common good.

I don't know what your destiny will be, but one thing I know—the only ones among you who will be really happy are those who have sought and found how to serve."

Albert Schweitzer

Source Notes

In this section, you will find the sources used in the real-life stories of this book.

1. *The First One Up . . .* (p. 11)
   – ABC News, 20/20, "Over a Barrel—The Truth about Oil," air date 07/24/09

2. *Can I Come to Your Party?* (p. 21, 22)
   – www.pacebutler.com/blog/recycling–facts/
   – www.professorshouse.com (article title "Why recycle plastic")
   – www.myzerowaste.com
   – www.greeninc.blogs.nytimes.com/2007/08
   – www.greatgarbagepatch.org

3. *Are You Thirsty?* (p. 29, 30, 31)
   - www.epa.gov/safewater/standards.html
   - National Geographic, Green Guide magazine, Summer 2008.
   - World Vision, print materials, 2009

4. *Precious Cargo?* (p. 39)
   - www.unmillenniumproject.org

5. *Ah, the Simple Egg* (p. 45, 46, 48)
   - www.greatgarbagepatch.org

6. *Margaret's Thanksgiving Turkey* (p. 60)
   - New York Times, 5/18/2008, "One Country's Table Scraps, Another Country's Meal"

7. *Dad's Trees* (p. 78, 79)
   - Andrew Lessman Vitamins, HSN, 1-800-284-3100 or HSN.com
   - Aveda, Aveda.com, 1-800-328-0849

8. *The Big Lake* (p. 84, 86, 88)
   - www.great-lakes.net
   - www.law.umkc.edu/faculty/projects
   - www.conservation.org/StopTheClock
   - www.nationalgeographic.com (ref. Oct 6, 2008)

9. *Science for All of Us ...* (p. 99, 101)
   - www.greatschools.org (Action for Education)
   - www.stevespangler.com (article title – "Science 'left behind' in American Schools")

Biography

> "I will not allow my life's light to be determined by the darkness around me."
> *Sojourner Truth*

Karen Olson Johnson is a well-known and highly respected public speaker and workshop presenter on sustainability topics and science. She has educated and inspired preschool through college level students in exciting hands-on science. She is a teachers' teacher who has taught hundreds of undergraduate and graduate level teachers-to-be as well as those with years of teaching experience. As a consultant, writer, and sustainability expert who develops science and environmental projects, Karen is much in demand. She delivers high-quality work tailored to the individual, group, or institution she serves.

A major way in which she lives out her passion for sustainability and justice issues is as a consociate of the Sisters of St. Joseph of Carondelet, St. Paul, Minnesota.

Born in one of those tiny blink-and-you'll-miss-it towns in Wisconsin and raised in Minnesota, she now lives in Minnesota with her husband.

For CVJ, SKO, and KGO